DISMISSED

To Esquire

LAW SCHOOL SURVIVAL

GUIDE

FOREWORD

I'm Nija Anise Bastfield, Esq., and yes, that 'Esquire' still hits differently. In 2014, I hit rock bottom: academically dismissed from the University of Baltimore School of Law with a 1.89 GPA. Devastated doesn't even cover it - I felt like a failure and worthless. But I didn't stay there. After my appeal was denied and the Appeals Board questioned my worthiness, I kept reapplying to the University of Baltimore School of Law, facing rejection after rejection. I quit for a moment - until Fall 2018, when I applied to the University of the District of Columbia David A. Clarke School of Law. By Fall 2019, after their Jump Start Program, I was starting as a Fall 2019 part-timer. This book is for students like me. When you flunk a test, battle imposter syndrome, or even fail out like I did, know this: your dream isn't dead. I'm proof you can rise and claim that 'Esquire' too.

TABLE OF CONTENTS

Contents

CHAPTER 1

I Finished My First Year Of Law School, Now What?

1L is a beast—everyone's got a guide for that. But what about 2L, 3L, or even 4L? If you're still standing after your first year, you're probably wondering, "How do I keep going?" That's where this guide comes in.

The transition into your second year is a real shift. Suddenly, the handholding is gone. The tutoring emails, exam workshops, and academic support feel like they've evaporated overnight. Professors assume you've got it down—but let's be real, none of us have it all figured out.

After 1L, I had to reassess my "why." Initially, I entered law school to prove something—to myself, to society, to everyone who doubted me. But surviving dismissal and rejection reshaped everything. I realized I was here to fight for kids like me—those the system counts out before they even get a chance.

Find your "why." It's not just motivation—it's your anchor when the grind gets heavy. Your "why" is what pulls you through when the outlines are endless, the stress feels unbearable, and the support systems fade.

And know this: you matter, and you deserve to be here. After 1L, law school can feel lonely. You become the older sibling—forgotten, expected to be okay even when you're not. People assume you've got it handled, but that doesn't mean you don't need help. Ask for it. Advocate for yourself. You are not alone in this.

CHAPTER 2

You Better Focus On "You!"

Law school will drain you—trust me, I've been there. In Fall 2022, my Tax Clinic Professor, Sakinah Tillman, flipped the script with meditation sessions and self-care talks. It was a game-changer when I was drowning in assignments and life. Self-care isn't selfish - it's survival. Here's how I learned to prioritize my mental, physical, and spiritual health. At the beginning of class, she held meditation sessions, and we even had guest speakers on emotional intelligence and self-care. I must say I wish I knew about these tips throughout my law school career, but I must admit it came at the right time when I was juggling a million assignments, roles, extracurricular activities, friends, family members, and personal and professional life.

Looking at the current state of the "millennial" type of life, we listen to podcasts, and oh boy do we listen to podcasts, but have you ever thought to listen to one that could motivate your life personally and not just for entertaining purposes? That is something that we should consider moving forward, especially as law students.

Mental Health

I know this goes without saying, but your mental health matters especially during law school. Mental health refers to your psychological, social, and emotional well-being and will surely be challenged during your law school journey. IT will test your dedication and ability to withstand discomfort.... and stress will be at an all-time high. Consequently, it will be imperative for you to remain vigilant on the state of your mental well-being.

"Dr. Jessica Miller DNP, MPH of Onsite Psychiatry LLC states that law school is a period where your mental and emotional health are especially vulnerable due to increased stress and expectations—making it vital to prioritize healthy routines, stay consistent with treatment, and protect your well-being just as you would your physical health."

Research shows that stress can negatively impact our mental state and cause a wear-and-tear effect on our emotional and mental capacity. Just like physical health there are actionable steps we can take to maintain good mental health hygiene such as scheduling time to exercise, ensuring we eat balanced meals, and prioritizing quality sleep as much as possible.

Additionally, if you have a known mental health diagnosis, making sure you are taking your prescribed medications and seeing your therapist regularly will be important - more on this later.

Remember, law school is a time when your mental and emotional being is more vulnerable due to the increased stress and expectations; treat yourself as such.

Spend time checking in with your emotions daily to see where you stand, be intentional about allowing yourself mental and physical downtime to just be, and give yourself grace when you don't do great on an exam. All these things positively impact your mental state.

If you're struggling with your mental health, please don't hesitate to reach out to your family, friends, or local mental health resources. 988 is a crisis and suicidal hotline available 24/7 to help you with any mental health emergency. Sometimes the strongest thing we can do is ask for help.

Therapy

Growing up Black, therapy wasn't a thing—prayer was. But when law school broke me, I needed more. My first session gave me steps I could actually use, and finding a therapist who looked like me? Priceless. Check your school or insurance, it's closer than you think. Once I got older, I realized that prayer did in fact work, but I needed more. I needed some true, actionable steps and guidance. I remember attending my first therapy session and feeling so relieved that I was given actionable tasks on how to address issues in my life. Think about it? We are all in our own respective professions and have achieved degrees and some even licenses, so why not speak to those who are experienced, well-versed, and even licensed in this area? The best part of all of this is that it is often offered at your law schools or through your health insurance companies.

You can tailor your search by gender, need, demographics, etc. That really helped me because I was able to select someone who looked just like me.

Spiritual

Spirituality is defined as a feeling and meaning that is something held close to your heart. Serving others reminded me why I was fighting for this degree. When thinking of the legal field and its inadequacy, I reflect on the difference that I can make in someone's life or even in society. I ponder on myself, my securities and insecurities, and define life as a situational experience where a person needs a source as a legal mediator between spiritual and discerning direction and educational comprehension. People often look at a Lawyer as a career position that pays a lot of money and comes with prestige and status.

As a child, I wanted to be a pediatrician, but at some point in my growth, my passion for law and the ability to make a difference for someone who needs legal advice and support changed that. Once I recognized that it was my true calling, trust me, the road was not easy, very challenging, and disheartening at times, due to financial and social roadblocks. There were times when giving up would have been easier, but something within me wouldn't let me. I now know that was my spiritual guidance. Nothing short of prayer and focusing on goodwill for others became my catalyst. Studying long days and nights, giving up on a real social life, became my existence.

With that being said, I found myself focusing on my spiritual walk with God and not on the lack of life process that my friends were embarking on. I knew I was thinking differently, I knew things were working in a new direction for me, but still on course in law school. It was an equilibrium. Without knowing it, my life became engulfed in church and youth ministry! Little did I know this would be a significant step in my journey to success. I was being guided by a higher power in a way that was misunderstood. Working with the youth, listening to their challenges, offering them support, guidance, gave me the comfort to recognize how fragile and valuable human life was, and I was identified as the Leader of the most important vessel in society, "children and youth," the "future!" For me, law became about more than prestige—it was the purpose. Working with youth in the ministry showed me why I couldn't quit.

Your spirit is what carries you when the books don't. My support and choices would make or break a human spirit or life's dreams and goals. My studying became easier, and my time became valued, my being became lighter. I recognized putting my spiritual journey first was the catalyst for my success.

My legal journey encompassed stepping out on faith for more expansive legal opportunities, working for less than my financial worth! All accepted as steps to my Promise!

CHAPTER 3

Relationships

As Black and brown law students, we often feel like we have something to prove. We walk into rooms already carrying the weight of assumptions, stereotypes, and pressure to succeed. But here's the truth: relationships can level the playing field. They're not just important, they're essential.

One narrative I've heard too often from employers and even professors is that law students aren't "professional." That we don't know how to carry ourselves. Let's be clear: we are professionals, and we absolutely belong here. But we also chose to step into a world that's historically excluded us. That took courage—and now we must be intentional about building relationships that sustain us.

Professional Relationships

Networking isn't about collecting business cards or building bonds.

I made it a goal to grab coffee with a mentor every month. Not because I needed something right away, but because when opportunities came up, I was at the top of mind. That's the power of genuine connection.

Here's what I want you to remember: people aren't stepping stones. They're people. If someone only contacted you when they needed something, how would that make you feel? Exactly.

So don't be that law student who files away a business card for graduation day, thinking "Oh, I remember someone in sports law!" but hasn't reached out in two years. Instead, be the student who sends the follow-up email, checks in occasionally, and builds a real connection over time

Faculty Relationships

Let me say this aloud: relationships with your professors matter—a lot.

Too often, we're afraid to admit we don't know something. We hesitate to ask questions or attend office hours because we don't want to seem unprepared. But the listening faculty remembers who shows up. When it's time to assign final grades, they remember the student who engaged in class, asked thoughtful questions, and came to office hours.

I once bumped my grade from a B+ to an A- because I consistently showed up and engaged. One conversation—one office hour visit—can tip the scale. Don't miss that.

And beyond grades, professors become recommenders, connectors, and even mentors. Nurture those relationships. They can open doors you didn't even know existed.

CHAPTER 4

Networking: Building Your Legal Tribe

Law school isn't just about mastering case law and constitutional doctrine—it's about building your people. Your tribe. The folks who'll vouch for you, uplift you, connect you, and challenge you to grow.

Networking isn't schmoozing—it's survival. Especially for Black and brown law students who may not have legacy connections or firm partners in the family, your tribe becomes your lifeline. And it's not about who you know, it's about who knows you.

Communication

Let's get straight to it: clarity is everything. Whether you're at a mixer or emailing a potential mentor, you need to be direct and intentional.

Have a 30-second elevator pitch ready:

"Hi, I'm [Your Name], a 1L at [School], with an interest in [e.g., environmental justice]. I'd love to learn how you approach [specific issues or fields]."

Keep emails tight—three sentences max:

"Hi [Name], I really appreciated your insights during the panel at [event]. I'd love to connect for a quick coffee chat to learn more about your work in [practice area]. Thank you!"

Rehearse it. Test it on a friend. Even get your mom to read it—mine's the best proofreader I've ever had. The goal is to make your communication clear, confident, and respectful.

And here's a practical tip for legal writing and editing: color-code your memorandums. I used CREAC, highlighting the Conclusion in blue, the Rule in green, and the Explanation/Application in red. It's a game-changer for organizing your thoughts and editing your flow.

Professionalism

Every time you engage—whether in person or online—you're auditioning for your future role as a lawyer.

Zoom calls? Dress like it matters. Business casual is the minimum—skip the bonnet and the hoodie.

In-person? Give a firm handshake, keep eye contact, and don't scroll through your phone during conversations.

And always follow through. If you say you'll send your resume or follow up, do it that day.

Quick story:

At a Professionalism Panel hosted by my Tax Clinic professor, I connected with the Honorable Judge Brandes Ash. After the event, I sent a simple email:

Greetings Judge Ash,

My name is Nija Bastfield. It was a pleasure reading your biography at our law school's Professionalism Panel. I'm a 4th-year evening law student graduating in May 2023, and I'd love to connect about navigating post-grad opportunities, if your schedule permits.

Best,

Nija A. Bastfield

She responded immediately and scheduled a FaceTime call with me. That conversation changed my life. Out of all the students who attended that panel, I was the only one who reached out. That moment led directly to my first post-grad opportunity as a Judicial Law Clerk at the Superior Court of the District of Columbia.

Don't underestimate a follow-up. Don't underestimate you.

How to Find Events

Start close: your school's career services, student orgs like BLSA, and school-wide panels are goldmines.

Go beyond school: check out local bar associations, state bar mixers, or national events like the ABA's Annual Meeting or NALP conferences.

Virtual's fair game too—LinkedIn Live Q&As, law firm webinars, and #LawTwitter convos. Set Google Alerts for legal networking events in your city.

And yeah, we use Eventbrite for brunches—so why not use it to build your career too?

Post-Event Contact

Follow up within 48 hours—no exceptions.

Handwritten notes are classy, but a clean, professional email works:

"Hi [Name], it was great connecting with you at [event]. Your story about [specific topic] really stayed with me—would love to connect again soon to hear more about your journey."

Add them on LinkedIn—with a personalized message.

"It was a pleasure meeting you at [event]! Looking forward to staying in touch."

And here's the key: don't ghost. Even a "Hey, things are hectic, let's circle back in a few weeks" keeps the connection alive.

I know a 3L who got a job because she followed up with a partner who'd completely forgotten their convo. She reminded him—he admired her follow-through—and boom, job secured.

Expand Your Reach

Local: Coffee chats with alumni, career office connections, or open house events.

State: Mock trial watch-parties, CLE workshop judges and practitioners attend these.

National: ABA meetings, specialty summits (e.g., IP, Sports, Criminal Law). Scholarships exist—apply early.

Virtual: Join niche webinars, slide into LinkedIn DMs (respectfully), attend firm Q&As. One DM I sent after a panel landed me a mentor in immigration law.

Your tribe won't always look like you, but they'll believe in you. So go build it. It might just change your career—and your life.

CHAPTER 5

Internships: Your Foot In The Door

Law school teaches theory. Internships teach reality. Whether you're dreaming of a courtroom, a corporate office, or a cause, internships bridge the gap between what you read and what you do. They're your early legal reps—and they matter.

This chapter will help you map out the options, land the position, and maximize the experience—because internships aren't just résumé boosters. They're proof that you belong.

Public Sector

Public internships are all about purpose. Think: court systems, District Attorney's offices, Public Defenders, legal aid clinics, or government agencies like the EPA or DOJ.

These gigs might not pay, but they pay off. You'll do real work—drafting motions, shadowing court appearances, researching actual policy—not just coffee runs and filing. And because these places are often understaffed, you'll gain hands-on experience early.

Story: A friend of mine interned at a Public Defender's office and was arguing a bail motion by week three. That's not happening in Big Law.

Apply early. These positions fill up fast. Check sites like USAJobs.gov, your state judiciary's internship listings, or your law school's public interest resource center.

Private Sector

This includes Big Law (like Skadden or Sidley), boutique firms (like IP or entertainment law), or in-house legal teams at companies like Meta or Nike.

Private internships tend to be high-pressure but pay high. You might sit in on depositions, proofread client memos, or research case law for ongoing litigation. Every detail counts. You're expected to dress the part, think fast, and write well.

Story: A 2L I know secured a Big Law offer by casually referencing a firm case in an interview. That prep work set her apart—and she got the job.

Tailor everything. No generic cover letters. Mention firm-specific cases or partners. Use Lexis or the firm's website to prep. Show you your homework—because they'll expect it.

Non-Traditional Paths

The law reaches way beyond courtrooms. You could intern with:

- Nonprofits (e.g., ACLU, NAACP Legal Defense Fund)
- Legal tech companies (like Clio or Case text)
- Sports and entertainment agencies
- Startups and advocacy groups

These roles value passion and creativity more than GPA. You might help draft contracts, write blog content, interview clients, or develop tools to make law more accessible.

Story: I became interested in sports law during my first clerkship. I got on LinkedIn and searched for folks connected to "MLB," "NFLPA," "NBPA," and "WNBPA." I cold messaged every one of them. Most didn't reply—but one did. That one connection led to a deep conversation, resources, and insight into an entirely new field. Sometimes, all it takes is one yes.

Use Your Career Office (Seriously)

Your career development office is more than just résumé templates and suit drives. They've got job boards (Symplicity, anyone?), alumni contacts, and leads on positions that never even get posted.

Book a one-on-one session. Practice your interview answers. Get feedback on your application materials. And don't be shy—ask them to connect you with alumni at firms, agencies, or courts you're targeting.

Story: During my second clerkship, I was searching for post-grad work in Baltimore. I cold emailed nearly every firm in the city with my résumé, cover letter, and transcript. One lawyer at Gordon Feinblatt responded—not because they were hiring, but because she respected my hustle.

That conversation led to an invite to a judicial reception, where I reconnected with old contacts and built new ones. Closed mouths don't get fed.

Quick Tips

- Be bold. Cold email. DM. Walk up to people at events. Be professional—but go for it.

- Say yes to unpaid gigs (if you can swing it). Sometimes the connections are worth more than the check.

- Keep a journal. Track what you liked, didn't like, and who you met. That info will help you later.

Internships are your legal playground. Explore, experiment, and be open to paths you didn't consider. Every conversation, every research memo, every awkward first-day moment is shaping your legal identity.

CHAPTER 6

Hit the Books: Become an Expert

Law school rewards depth, not dabbling. It's easy to skim cases just enough to limp through class—but mastery happens when you dive deep. This chapter shows you how to own a subject so completely that you become the go-to resource in your section.

Choose Your Niche

Each semester, pick one area to specialize in—First Amendment, secured transactions, tax law, whatever intrigues you. Your goal isn't to become a mini professor in every subject, but to have one domain where you're undeniably confident.

- Why it matters: Professors notice depth. During cold calls, you'll speak with authority. Classmates will come to you with questions. And when it's time for recommendations or study groups, you'll be first on the list.

- How to pick: Consider what lights you up. Which classes leave you curious? Which hypotheticals do you want to argue? Follow that spark.

Deep Reading, Not Skimming

Casebook excerpts are just the start. Real understanding comes from reading full opinions on Westlaw or Lexis:

1. Read the majority and dissent. Dissents often unveil policy debates and alternative frameworks—gold for class discussions.

2. Annotate vigorously. In the margins, note policy insights, cross-references to other cases, and personal reactions.

3. Summarize in your own words. After reading, write a one-paragraph summary without legalese. If you can't, reread until you can.

Leverage Secondary Sources

Supplements aren't cheating—they're tools. Use concise hornbooks (e.g., Examples & Explanations) or treatises to clarify complexity:

- Blogs & Newsletters: SCOTUS blog, TaxProf Blog, and the Volokh Conspiracy keep you current on hot topics.

- Podcasts: Strict Scrutiny for constitutional law, Tax Notes Talk for tax—listen during commutes or workouts.

- Law Review Articles: Pick one recent article in your niche each month. Read the introduction and conclusion to gauge relevance, then dive in if it excites you.

Active Learning Techniques

Passive reading won't cut it. Engage actively:

- Flashcards & Spaced Repetition: Use Anki to drill key rules, elements, and policy rationales.

- Teach a Peer: Explaining the rule against perpetuities to a study buddy cements your grasp.
- Mind Maps: Draw concept maps linking doctrines—e.g., under Contracts, map offer, acceptance, consideration, defenses. Visual links stick.

Bringing Current Events into Class

Connect doctrine to headlines. If you're in Constitutional Law and there's a new Supreme Court decision on free speech, mention it in discussion. If you follow a regulatory change in tax, reference it in class. Real-world connections show professors you're not just studying for grades—you're preparing for practice.

Prep for Cold Calls

Cold calls terrify everyone—but preparation eases the sting:

1. Outline likely questions. After each case, jot down potential hypotheticals.
2. Practice aloud. Verbally run through your answers, not just in your head.
3. Have a structure. Start with the rule, apply facts, then conclude. "Rule–Application–Conclusion" is your mantra.

Build a "Knowledge Vault"

Keep a running document for your niche:

- Headnotes: Brief summaries of key cases.
- Policy Notes: Bullet points on why rules exist.

- Hypo Bank: Create 2–3 hypotheticals per rule to test yourself.

Review this vault weekly. It's your secret weapon come exam time.

Mastery is magnetic. When you speak with confidence, professors notice—and doors open: research assistant gigs, recommendation letters, leadership roles in journals. Become that expert. Law school isn't a mile wide and an inch deep—it's a marathon of mastery.

CHAPTER 7

Grades: Aim High

Your grades aren't your identity—but in law school, they're your currency. They open doors to clerkships, coveted internships, and prestigious post-grad roles. So, let's set a target above "pass" and build the habits to hit it.

Set a Clear Goal

Top 20%? Top 10%? Decide where you want to land. Specific goals drive specific actions:

- "I will rank in the top 15% of my 2L class."
- "I will earn at least one A in a major course this semester."

Write your goal somewhere you'll see daily—your planner, phone wallpaper, or study nook.

Reverse-Engineer Your Exam

If exams are 100% of your grade, treat them like projects:

1. Gather past exams. Check your professor's office, the law library, or student groups.
2. Identify the hot topics. Look for patterns: property disputes, contract breaches, constitutional hypos.
3. Outline model answers. Draft thesis statements, rule statements, and sample analyses for each issue.

When you know what "excellent" looks like, you can aim directly at it.

Daily Study Habit

Consistency beats cramming every time:

- 2–3 hours daily of focused study outside class.
- Break sessions into 50-minute blocks with 10-minute breaks.
- Mix subjects to prevent burnout—Contracts Monday, Torts Tuesday, etc.

Structure your day like a job: show up, work the plan, log off. Your brain will thank you.

Practice, Practice, Practice

- **Practice Exams:** Simulate test conditions. Time yourself, silence your phone, and sit at a desk.
- **Problem Sets:** Do hypos from supplements or past classes. Treat each like a mini exam.
- **Feedback Loop:** After each practice, spend as much time reviewing mistakes as answering questions.

Record wrong answers in a "Book of Wrongs" with the rule, why you missed it, and how to fix it.

Study Groups—Use Wisely

Not all group study is productive. To level up:

1. Small Group (2–3 people). Too many voices dilute focus.
2. Roles & Agenda: One briefs cases, one drafts hypos, one challenges with questions—rotate weekly.
3. Accountability: Set goals ("Today, we outline the negligence tort elements") and stick to them.

A sharp group can catch what you miss. A loose group can waste hours.

Office Hours & Professor Engagement

Grades aren't just about exams, they're about impressions:

- Visit office hours with specific questions. "On the MEE, how deeply should I analyze policy under the rule against perpetuities?" beats "Can you help me?"
- Demonstrate growth. Show your draft outline and ask how to deepen the analysis.
- Follow up. Send a brief thank-you email summarizing what you learned—keeps you memorable.

Those interactions can be the tiebreaker between an A- and a B+.

Self-Care for Peak Performance

High grades require a healthy you:

- Sleep: 7+ hours nightly. Pulling all-nighters may backfire.
- Exercise: Even a 20-minute walk improves focus and mood.
- Nutrition: Brain fuel matters—lean proteins, fruits, veggies, hydration.

When your body and mind are aligned, learning sticks.

Mindset: Growth Over Fixed

Law school is a learning curve, not a tournament you're doomed to lose:

- **Embrace mistakes.** Each wrong answer is data for your next study session.
- **Celebrate small wins.** An improved practice exam score, a succinct rule statement—recognize progress.
- **Stay curious.** See each class as an opportunity, not an obligation.

Aim high, study smart, and protect your well-being. Your grades will follow—and with them, the opportunities you've earned.

CHAPTER 8

Studying: Where, How, When

Studying law isn't about logging in for endless hours; it's about matching where, how, and when to your unique focus rhythms and learning style. Here's your blueprint for maximum retention with minimum wasted grind:

Where: Find Your Focus Zone

- Library Carrel: Silent, structured, academic vibe. Ideal for dense doctrine (Constitutional Law, Tax).
- Coffee Shop Nook: Ambient buzz fuels energy. Great for active tasks—flashcards, outlines, podcast listening.
- Home Office: Comfort meets control. Block distractions (use website blockers), keep your desk clear, and reserve this spot for creative work—brief writing, mind mapping.
- Study Rooms: Group-friendly spaces for hypos and discussions. Reserve in advance.

Pro tip: Test each environment for 1–2 sessions. Track your productivity ("Did I finish that outline?"). Then pick your go-to spot for each task type.

How: Active Over Passive

1. **Active Recall:** Close the book and recite rules, elements, and policy rationales out loud.

2. **Spaced Repetition:** Use Anki or paper flashcards. Review rules Day 1, Day 3, Day 7, Day 14.

3. **Interleaving:** Mix subjects within a session. Don't do four hours of only Contracts—rotate Contracts, Torts, Property in 50-minute blocks.

4. **Self-Explanation:** After reading a case, explain its holding and reasoning to an imaginary 12-year-old. Simple language reveals gaps.

5. **Practice Hypos:** Draft mini essays under timed conditions. Even one issue at a time (e.g., negligence duty) builds speed.

When: Sync with Your Energy

- **Morning Peak (7–11 a.m.):** Tackle hardest tasks—deep reading, case analysis, drafting outlines.

- **Afternoon Slump (1–4 p.m.):** Reserve for review—flashcards, podcasts, supplement summaries.

- **Evening Focus (8–11 p.m.):** Perfect for group study, hypos, and reviewing the day's notes.

- **Weekend Marathons:** One 3-hour block for cumulative outlining; one block for practice exams.

Structuring Your Study Week

Day	Morning	Afternoon	Evening
Monday	Deep read Contracts	Flashcards & Anki review	Group hypo session
Tuesday	Property case analysis	Podcast on current events	Rewrite class notes
Wednesday	Torts outline drafting	Supplement reading (E&E)	Solo hypos (30 min each)
Thursday	Constitutional Law deep-dive	Flashcards & review	Office hours prep
Friday	Review "Knowledge Vault"	Practice exam question	Light review/rest
Saturday	Full practice exam (3 hrs)	Review "Book of Wrongs"	Free/social time
Sunday	Cumulative outline update	Planning next week's schedule	Self-care (meditation, walk)

Tools & Tech

- **Noise-Cancelling Headphones:** Block distractions anywhere.
- **Anki / Quizlet:** Spaced-repetition flashcards.

- **OneNote / Notion:** Organize cases, outlines, and hypos in searchable sections.
- **Forest App / Pomodoro Timer:** Enforce focused blocks and breaks.
- **Physical Planner:** Visualize weekly blocks; check off completed sessions.

Guarding Your Time

- Schedule study blocks as non-negotiable appointments.
- Batch small tasks (emailing study partners, printing outlines) into one 30-minute slot.
- Say "no" to extra commitments when your week is full.

Studying smart means matching the environment, method, and timing to your personal rhythm. With this structure, you'll learn more in less time—and keep your sanity intact.

CHAPTER 9

Classroom: Own the Stage

The classroom is your arena. It's where you transform from a bystander into a confident contributor. Stop surviving lectures—start commanding them. Here's how to prep, perform, and follow up so you leave every session one step ahead.

Pre-Class Preparation

1. TWO-PASS READING

Skim for Gist: Spend 10–15 minutes getting the overview—facts, procedural posture, key rule.

Deep Dive: Reread with focus. Brief the case:

- Facts: Who did what to whom?
- Issue: What question did the court answer?
- Rule: What law governs?
- Reasoning: Why did the court decide that way?
- Conclusion: How did it resolve the dispute?

2. USE A SUPPLEMENT

A short hornbook or outline (Examples & Explanations, Grip's Nutshell) can clarify confusing points. If a concept still trips you up, watch a 5-minute YouTube explainer or read a concise blog post.

3. PREPARE HYPO QUESTION

After briefing, jot 1–2 hypotheticals. Example: "If the defendant sold digital art instead of physical, does the same property rule apply?" These hypotheses prime your mind for class discussion.

In-Class Performance

- Mindset: You belong here. Professors want engagement. They'd rather hear a thoughtful "I don't know yet, but here's my reasoning" than silence.

- Cold Calls: Pause, take a breath, then structure your answer: Rule → Application → Conclusion. A quick "Let me gather my thoughts" is perfectly acceptable.

- Active Listening: Don't transcribe—synthesize. Note the professor's emphasis ("This policy matters because...") and any class-wide reactions.

- Strategic Participation: Aim for quality over quantity. One insightful comment trumps three half-baked ones. Tie your point back to the rule or policy.

Post-Class Review

- 24-Hour Rewrite: Within a day, rewrite your notes. Fill in gaps, clarify shorthand, and integrate any class insights.

- Group Debrief: Meet one or two classmates to compare notes and debate hypotheses. They'll catch what you missed; you'll solidify your understanding.

- Outline Integration: Add new rules, examples, and policy points to your master outline. Building it incrementally prevents end-of-semester panic.

Office Hours: Your Secret Weapon

- Come with Specifics: Don't just say, "I'm confused." Show your brief or outline and ask, "In this hypo, should I treat X like Y?"
- Listen & Record: Professors share gold—preferences on exams, nuances in doctrine, even career advice. Jot it down.
- Follow Up: A quick thank-you email ("Your insight on the statute of frauds example really clicked for me—thank you!") keeps you memorable and shows professionalism.

Essential Supplies

Item	Purpose
Laptop or tablet	Organized notes (OneNote/Notion)
Single-color highlighter	Emphasis without chaos
Sticky tabs	Mark key cases in your casebook
Noise-canceling earbuds	Block distractions before/after class
Water bottle & snacks	Maintain energy and focus.

Owning the classroom means showing up prepared, engaging with confidence, and reinforcing learning immediately afterward. Each session is an opportunity to stand out, deepen your grasp, and build the reputation that carries you beyond grades.

CHAPTER 10

Social: Work/Life Balance

Law school is a marathon, not a sprint. If you let it, it will consume you—your health, relationships, and joy. This chapter helps you carve out space for life, so you return to your studies energized, not empty.

Why Balance Matters

- Sustained Performance: Chronic stress kills focus. Regular breaks reboot your brain.
- Emotional Health: Friendships and hobbies remind you there's more to you than case law.
- Long-Term Success: Habits you build now carry into your legal career. Burnout in law school often predicts burnout as an associate.

Block Your Joy

Treat fun like a class:

Activity	Frequency	Time Block
Gym or exercise	3× per week	1 hour
Social outing	1× per week	2–3 hours
Downtime (TV, reading)	Daily	30–45 minutes
Spiritual/meditation	3× per week	20 minutes

Put these in your calendar. Honor them. If it's on the schedule, it happens.

The Power of "No"

You can't do everything. Every "yes" is a "no" to something else—sleep, study, self-care. Before you commit, ask:

- Does this align with my goals?
- Will it energize or drain me?
- Can I realistically fit it in?

It's okay to skip a club meeting or say no to an event. Protect your bandwidth.

Micro-Breaks & Transitions

- Pomodoro Breaks: After 50 minutes of study, take 10 minutes to stretch, hydrate, or step outside.
- Transition Ritual: Use a short ritual to shift between study and life—change your playlist, take a quick walk, or journal one sentence about your mood.

These rituals signal to your brain it's time to rest or refocus.

Maintain Relationships

Law school strains friendships and family ties. Keep connections strong:

- Weekly Check-Ins: A quick text or call with a friend or family member.

- Combine Social & Study: Invite a friend to join your study group or go for a "walk and talk" session.
- Be Present: When you're off the clock, really be off. Silence notifications, close your laptop, and engage fully.

Self-Care Toolbox

Self-Care Mode	Example Activities	Benefits
Physical	Yoga, gym, walking, dance	Energy, stress relief
Mental	Reading fiction, puzzles, games	Cognitive reset, fun
Emotional	Journaling, therapy, heart-to-hearts	Clarity, emotional release
Spiritual	Meditation, prayer, service	Purpose, grounding

Rotate through modes weekly. A balanced toolbox keeps you resilient.

Spotting Burnout

Warning signs:
- Chronic fatigue or insomnia
- Irritability or mood swings
- Loss of motivation or apathy
- Physical aches (headaches, back pain)

If you notice these, pause. Scale back study hours, lean into self-care, or seek support—counseling, peer groups, or mentors.

Integrate Passions

Don't abandon what you love. Whether it's painting, sports, or volunteering, find small ways to keep your passions alive. They recharge you and make you a more well-rounded lawyer.

Balance isn't a luxury—it's a necessity. By scheduling joy, setting boundaries, and practicing self-care, you'll not only survive law school; you'll thrive.

CHAPTER 11

Graduation: Now What?

Your last semester feels surreal—no more cases to brief, no more classes to attend. Yet the question looms: what comes next? This chapter helps you leverage your hard-won credentials, your network, and your resilience as you step from law student into lawyer.

1. Reflect & Clarify Your Goals

Before you dive into applications, pause and ask:

- What energizes me? Litigation? Policy? Advocacy? Corporate deals?

- What lifestyle do I want? Big city or small town? Firm hours or flexible schedule?

- What skills do I bring? Research, writing, negotiation, and technical aptitude?

Write a one-page "Career Mission Statement." It will guide your search and keep you focused when opportunities—and distractions—abound.

2. Mine Your Network ("Relation Back")

Your contacts fall into three tiers:

Tier	Who's In It	How to Leverage
1	Professors, mentors, and former employers	Ask for referrals, recommendations
2	Classmates, study-group peers, student-org alumni	Share leads, co-apply, mock interviews
3	Event contacts, LinkedIn connections, and cold emails that responded	Re-introduce yourself, request advice calls

Action Steps:

1. List everyone you've connected with (class, events, internships)
2. Prioritize by closeness and relevance to your goals.

Reach out with a personalized message: "I'm graduating in May and exploring [field]. Would you be open to a 15-minute chat about your experience at [organization]?"

Closed mouths don't get fed—keep asking.

3. Leverage School Resources

- Career Services: They have unadvertised job leads, alumni mentors, and mock interview slots.

- Alumni Platform: Many schools host databases—filter by geography, practice area, employer
- On-Campus Interviews (OCI): Even if Big Law isn't your dream, treat OCI like practice for real interviews.
- Be proactive: schedule appointments early, prepare tailored materials, and follow up promptly.

4. Craft Targeted Applications

- Tailor Your Resume & Cover Letter: Highlight relevant clinic work, leadership roles, and standout achievements. Mirror language from the job posting.
- Show Impact: Use metrics ("drafted 10+ motions," "managed pro bono caseload of 15 clients") and concrete outcomes.
- Express Fit: In your letter, connect your "why" (Chapter 1) to the organization's mission.

5. Nail the Interview

- Research Deeply: Know recent cases, deals, or initiatives the employer handled.
- Prepare Stories: Use the STAR method—Situation, Task, Action, Result—for behavioral questions.
- Ask Insightful Questions: "How does your firm support junior lawyers in finding pro bono projects?" shows you've thought about culture and values.
- Follow Up: Send a brief thank-you email within 24 hours, referencing a specific discussion point.

6. Consider Transitional Roles

Your first job isn't forever. If your ideal role isn't immediate:

- Temp Agencies & Contract Roles: Gain experience, build references, and earn income.

- Fellowships & Clerkships: Judicial clerkships or public interest fellowships can be springboards.

- Staff Attorney Positions: Nonprofit or government roles often hire new grads and offer meaningful work.

7. Manage the Emotional Shift

Graduation brings excitement—and loss. You're leaving a structured world and a community you've known.

- Rituals: Commencement ceremonies, dinners with classmates, or personal rituals (writing a letter to your 1L self).

- Stay Connected: Schedule periodic check-ins with study buddies or mentors.

- Set New Routines: Replace class schedules with professional routines—dedicated work hours, networking goals, and continued learning.

8. Lifelong Learning Mindset

Law school taught you to learn. Now:

- CLE & Certifications: Identify required continuing-education credits and consider specializations (e.g., mediation, cybersecurity law).

- Reading Habit: Subscribe to industry newsletters, legal blogs, and relevant journals.
- Professional Groups: Join bar-section committees, affinity groups, or in-house legal networks.

9. Give Back

You've received mentorship, resources, and support. Pay it forward:

- Mentor 1Ls & 2Ls: Host a coffee chat, review resumes, or share your story.
- Pro Bono: Volunteer with legal aid clinics or community organizations.
- Guest Speak: Offer to speak at your law school or local bar events.
- Giving back cements your learning, expands your network, and honors your journey.

You've earned your Esquire. Graduation is not an endpoint but a launchpad. Armed with clarity, connections, and confidence, you're ready to shape your legal career—and make an impact. Go forth and thrive.

CHAPTER 12

Bar Exam Prep

Passing the bar is your ultimate comeback story. You've conquered dismissal, rejection, and law school's grind—now it's time to turn that dedication into a license. Here's how to prep like it's a game day, protect your relationships, and build the skills you need to pass.

1. Choose Your Program—Strategically

You'll hear endless endorsements: Themis, Barbri, Kaplan, Helix, and more. Each caters to different learning styles:

- Structured Lectures: Barbri or Themis—daily videos, tight schedules.

- Adaptive Learning: Adaptibar for MBE practice; Helix for personalized pathways.

- Flexibility: Kaplan's on-demand library; private tutors for bespoke plans.

- Action: Use free trials. Attend sample classes.

Match the format to your study habits. If you need one-on-one attention, budget for a tutor or tap alumni networks for affordable options.

2. Build a Game-Day Schedule

Treat bar prep like a job—because it is. Draft a daily schedule that accounts for:

- Study Blocks: 8–10 hours/day, broken into 2–3-hour focused sessions.
- Essentials: Meals, exercise, sleep, and brief social time.
- Buffer Zones: Extra review or catch-up slots.
- Template: Start with your bar program's mock schedule. Customize it around your peak energy times. Post it where you see it every day.

3. Protect Your Relationships

- Bar prep strains bonds—plan ahead:
- Transparent Conversations: Tell family/friends your availability and response times.
- Scheduled Check-Ins: One brief weekly call or coffee to maintain support.
- Group Study Dates: Combine social time with study—quiz each other over brunch. Clear expectations prevent resentment.

4. Master the MBE (Multistate Bar Exam)

- Questions, Questions, Questions: Adaptibar is gold for drilling. Aim for 200–300 MBE questions/week.
- Book of Wrongs: For every missed question, log the topic, correct rule, and your error. Review weekly.

- Topic Blitz: Each week, focus on one subject (e.g., Torts Week, Evidence Week). Do 50–100 questions in that area, then review.

5. Conquer the MPT (Performance Test)

Many overlook the MPT—big mistake. It's practical and predictable:

- File Simulation: Treat it like a real client folder. Inventory the facts, identify tasks (memo, brief, letter).
- Practice Past MPTs: Available on state board websites (e.g., NY, MN). Aim for 1–2 per week.
- Template Library: Build issue-spotting and organization templates. Familiarity saves time.

6. Dominate the MEE (Essays)

- Timed Essays: Simulate exam conditions—30 minutes per essay, no exceptions.
- IRAC/CREAC Mastery: Write one rule statement, one application paragraph, and one conclusion
- Issue Checklist: For each subject, maintain a checklist of common issues (e.g., statute of fraud, self-defense). Quick scan before writing.
- Resources: State board sites, SmartBarPrep, past essay compilations.

7. Review & Self-Assessment

- Weekly Simulations: Full morning (MBE) + afternoon (MEE/MPT) session.
- Performance Tracking: Chart scores. Identify weak subjects. Adjust your schedule.
- Peer Review: Swap essays with a study partner. Critique structure, analysis, clarity.

8. Self-Care During Bar Prep

- Sleep Priority: 7+ hours/night. No all-nighters.
- Movement Breaks: 5–10-minute stretch every hour.
- Mindfulness: Short meditation or breathing exercises daily.
- Nutrition: Balanced meals; limit caffeine crashes.

9. Logistics & Final Prep

- Exam Day Kit: IDs, snacks, water, permitted equipment. Pack it a week early.
- Venue Recon: Visit the test center beforehand. Know the route, parking, and entry rules.
- Mental Rehearsal: Visualize the day—walking in, sitting down, tackling Qs calmly.

Passing the bar is more than knowledge—it's endurance, strategy, and self-management. You've survived law school's toughest battles. Now you'll conquer the bar. Let's go claim that, Esquire.

Struggling with Law School?

Don't let challenging concepts hold you back. We offer comprehensive tutoring services designed to help you succeed in law school. Whether you're having trouble with Contracts, Torts, Criminal Law, or any other Subject, our experienced tutors can provide the support you need.

We Offer:

- Personalized Tutoring
- Exam Preparation
- Essay Writing Assistance
- Concept Clarification
- Case Briefing Strategies
- Time Management Skills

Why Choose Us?

- **Customized Approach:** We tailor our tutoring to your individual needs.
- **Flexible Scheduling:** We offer convenient tutoring times to fit your busy schedule.
- **Proven Results:** Our students consistently achieve higher grades and pass the bar exam.

Ready to take your law school performance to the next level?
BastfieldConsulting@outlook.com

DEAR WORLD

First, I would like to give all glory and honor to God because without him, I would not be where I am today. Often, I prayed in the shower to place me in a position where I can use my license to help God's people, and I am certain that this is just one of those ways that I can help touch or even motivate a law student's life. Thank you to everyone that I have crossed paths with over the years. I appreciate each person I met throughout this journey. You taught me things about myself, and you showed me that genuine people still exist in this hectic and mean world.

It is my hope that my book lands in the hands of every law student regardless of race, national origin, sexual orientation, gender, or social status. You got into law school, so you conquered half the battle. I cannot guarantee that my thoughts, suggestions, or words can help you throughout law school, but it is my hope that they help at least one of you, and then I would know that my writing was not in vain. To every law student: you're halfway there. If one tip here lifts you up, I've done my job.

Signing off,

Nija Anise Bastfield, Esq.
Larry & Pauline's Daughter

www.ingramcontent.com/pod-product-compliance
Lightning Source LLC
Chambersburg PA
CBHW031238120626
46545CB00003B/1172